DIARY
OF A
MINECRAFT
ZOMBIE

Book 4

Zack Zombie

Sunday

*C*ock-a-doodle-doo!

"Wake up, sleepy head, it's time to rise and shine!"

"Urrggghhhwwhuzzat?"

"I said, it's morning and time for you to get up."

Morning? Did my parents forget that Zombies burn in the daylight?

"Mom, that's not funny, I'm trying to sleep."

"Who are you calling Mom?"

"Wha…?!!"

Oh Man! It wasn't a dream. I really did swap bodies with Steve!

Now this villager is trying to get me out of bed early in the morning, and make me go out in the daylight.

I better play along so I won't give myself away.

"Hey, there...uh...Mr. Villager. What's going on...er...in your villager life?" I said.

"What's the matter with you, Steve? Did you get bit by a Zombie or something?"

"He, he... That's real funny, bro... He, he."

"Man, you're acting really weird this morning," he said.

So much for my acting skills.

But I'd better get good at it quick, because I'm going to have to act like Steve for the next few weeks until the full moon. That's when

2

the Swamp Witch that can switch our bodies back will come home.

I just have to remember what Steve told me.

I think he told me that to blend in with the humans, I just had to stick with the basics...

"Humans are simple," Steve said. "As long as you do what they do, you'll fit right in."

So, what does Steve do all day? Let me see...

I know that he likes mining, farming, and punching trees. I guess as long as I do those three things, I should fit right in.

But how am I going to learn how to do any of those things? I've never done them before!

Then a ray of sunshine came into my room.

At first I freaked out because I thought my skin would fry like bacon.

But then I realized that being Steve has its perks. I don't have to be afraid of the daylight anymore!

So, first thing I did was go out into the open field to take in all of the sunshine.

It felt really good on my face and body, but it was a little too bright.

I was able to see all of the fields, and the trees, and the lake…

The lake!

I just realized that I could jump in the water and swim!

Normally, Zombies avoid water like the plague.

But now, I can go in water like all the other humans.

So the next thing I did was run to the lake.

I climbed a really big tree and...
SSSPPPLLLAAASSSHHHH!

Didn't last long in the water though.

For some reason I thought humans could breathe under water... Cough, cough.

Later that evening I went to go visit Steve at our usual spot.

I could not believe my eyes!

Only one day into it, and Steve was already rockin' the Zombie life.

"How was your first day of Zombie life?" I asked him.

"Aw, Bro, Zombie life is really cool!" Steve said. "I could really get used to this."

"Really? I thought being a Zombie really stinks."

"Well, the smell is pretty bad, but I think I've gotten used to it by now," Steve said.

"How about you? How's it going living my old boring life? Have you met those crazy villagers yet?"

"Yeah, what's up with that?" I said. "I thought you lived with your parents."

"Well, you wouldn't believe this, but I don't know where I'm from," Steve said. "I've lived with the villagers all my life. I've never even met my parents."

"Didn't you ask the villagers where you're from?" I asked Steve.

"I did ask them," Steve said. "They just said that one day I woke in their bed, and they have no idea where I came from."

"Whoa."

"There's a lot of other stuff that's gonna weird you out, just wait."

"Like what?"

"You'll see," Steve said.

Then we went our separate ways.

Man, I never looked that cool when I was a Zombie.

How does he do that?

As soon as I got home, one of the villagers said, "Whoa, you stink. You need to go take a shower and get that rotten meat smell off of you. You smell like you were wrestling with a Zombie."

I actually liked smelling like my old self again.

So the villager handed me a bar of what he called "SO-AP," and handed me something called a "TA-WOOL," and then he told me to go take something called a "SHA-WUR." He pointed me to a place called the "BA-FROOM."

8

Man, I was getting dizzy just trying to remember it all.

As I walked into the BA-FROOM, I walked past the mirror and I had to do a double-take.

I got a chance to see my face, and boy was it weird.

I had eyeballs, a nose, ears, and I had skin everywhere. I also had bits of hair on my chin.

Then I opened my mouth and saw that I had like a million teeth! I looked like a shark.

Whoa. What does Steve do with all of these teeth, anyway?

I wonder if humans really do eat Zombies, like in the movies.

Maybe I could practice being like Steve. So I tried making different faces...

Man, I don't know if I'll be able to pull it off. But I'm going to try.

So after I took my SHA-WUR, I went to bed.

But I had a hard time sleeping because of my wet clothes.

Monday

"Steve, hurry up, or you're going to be late for school," the villager said.

Oh Man! Steve never mentioned anything about school!

I thought mining and farming was going to be hard, but trying to fit in at a human school is going to be impossible.

I mean, what do I wear? How do I act? What do I say to the other kids?

Will they even like me? What if they find out I'm really a Zombie in a Steve meat suit?

Man, I've only been a human for two days and my life is already filled with drama.

I looked in the closet for clothes to wear and I couldn't find any.

I looked in the drawers and found he had a bunch of the same shirts and a bunch of the same pants.

Man, I thought only Zombies did that.

So I grabbed a shirt and pair of pants to put on.

I had a hard time putting them on until the villager walked in on me.

"Are you trying to put on new clothes on top of your old clothes?" the villager said. "You act like you've never worn clothes before."

After he walked out of the room I took off my old clothes, and I couldn't believe what I saw…

Steve's skin totally covered his body!

He didn't have any holes, or patches where his guts hung out.

You couldn't reach in and play with his stomach, or his intestines, or his spine, like I could do with my Zombie body.

Man, this is weird, I thought.

Then I threw on some clothes and went to school.

The village during the day was intense!

There were villagers all over the place.

Villagers in black robes, villagers in white robes, villagers in purple robes, and more.

It was crazy!

It's a good thing that the school was in the village. It was real easy to find.

14

But I thought the village was crazy. School was even crazier!

There were all kinds of kids in this place. There were skinny ones, fat ones, tall ones, and short ones.

And these kids weren't wearing robes; they were wearing all kinds of crazy clothes.

One kid looked like he was wearing a porcupine on his head.

One girl looked like she used her face as a canvas for painting.

And there were a bunch of other kids that were almost as big as Mutant, but they had skin on them. I think they said they played a game called FOOT-BALL.

I even saw a Zombie at school!

But he had more meat on him than the usual living dead.

Maybe in Steve's world Zombies eat tons of cake.

The weirdest thing I saw was that all the kids hung out with just the kids that looked like them.

This was really different from my mob school back home.

All the mobs at my school hang out with different mob kids all the time.

That's why me, Skelee, Slimey, and Creepy are best friends.

But here, humans act really weird.

I think I'm going to go home early today...

Tuesday Morning

I was really weirded out by what I saw yesterday.

I mean, all those humans in one place gave me the creeps.

Not to mention, the smell!

Not one kid smelled like rotten flesh, or stale mucus, or moldy gym socks.

Except for one kid…who smelled like all three. I really liked him.

But, I decided that today, I was going to get through it.

I mean, Steve is probably having a tough time too.

Being a Zombie is really hard, you know. Especially trying to keep up with the cool lifestyle and reputation I've built for myself at school.

I feel real sorry for him.

The cool thing is that Steve gave me his extra cellphone so we can call each other in case we get in a sticky situation.

I'm probably going to call him like fifty times today.

Well, here goes another day of craziness at human middle school…

Tuesday Night

Today was the worst day of my life.

Man, I thought there was drama in being a Zombie.

These humans have drama, times ten!

As soon as I got to school today, all the other kids were looking at me and saying stuff to each other.

I wanted to be friendly, so I went up to one kid to say, "Hi." He did something with his eyes and walked away.

I didn't know you could roll your eyes into your head like that...

Then when I was walking to class, I tripped and accidentally dropped my books on the floor.

I was still getting used to walking straight.

I went to go pick my books up, but then everybody started kicking them down the hallway.

Somehow they ended up in the toilet bowl in the boy's bathroom.

The good thing is that now they actually smell like my books back home.

My first class was called "How to Annihilate Mobs and Eradicate Them From Existence."

It was taught by a former army sergeant that fought in the previous Zombie Apocalypse.

His name was Master Sergeant Fuller B. Loney.

All I can tell you is that all through class I was shaking like a leaf.

He talked about how to chop Zombies into little bits with a pickaxe or axe. But, he said, the best weapon is a sword. You can cut off arms and legs real easy with a sword.

I was about to hurl in the middle of class.

He said with creepers, you need to be really careful. The best assault is to knock them into other mobs so that they can blow up the whole lot.

Slimes are easy, he said. Just lure them into a lake and drown them.

But skeletons are the worst. He said you've got to either use TNT to blow up a bunch of them, or chop them down to size with a sword.

"And if you ever find yourself out of food..." he said, "You can use rotten flesh to make some great beef jerky. Zombie Jerky, I call it."

I blew out of class so fast, I left the door swinging behind me.

Right in the middle of the school hallway, I hurled.

All of the other kids started laughing at me, especially when I slipped and fell in my vomit.

I actually didn't mind the vomit…

The laughing, though, I didn't like very much.

The one good thing that happened today was that a really nice girl helped me and took me to get cleaned up.

"Are you OK, Steve?" she said.

"You know who I am?"

"Steve, it's me. Alex," she said. "You must've hit your head harder than I thought."

"Hi Alex," I said.

She took some paper towels and started cleaning the vomit off my face and clothes.

I asked her to leave a little on my shirt because the smell reminded me of home.

She just looked at me... Confused.

Well, after all that drama, I decided to go home early again, today.

Maybe tomorrow I can make it through a whole day of human school.

I seriously doubt it...

Wednesday

The villagers I live with look pretty smart with their long robes and big noses.

So, I thought I would ask them what I could do to fit in at school.

One of the villagers told me that if I want to fit in, then I need to find a group of kids that like what I like.

He said that's what all of the villagers do. The Farmers stick with the Farmers, the Librarians stick with the Librarians, the Blacksmiths stick with the Blacksmiths, the Priests stick with the Priests, and the Butchers stick with the Butchers.

He said that they all even dress the same.

That made a lot of sense, I thought.

So, today at lunch time, I decided to find a group of kids that like what I like.

The problem was that there were so many groups to choose from!

I was thinking of joining the FOOT-BALL players. But they were too big, and not very smart.

I thought about joining the girls with the painted faces. But they kept doing that "rolling your eyes" thing that really creeps me out.

I was thinking of joining the group of weird kids with glasses. But they were too busy playing with their mini-computers and protecting their pockets and stuff.

I know, I thought. I'll join the group of Zombie kids!

28

I heard they called themselves "Goths." I didn't know what that meant, but I knew the living dead when I saw them.

That's it! I thought. That's the group I'm going to be part of.

I decided to sit at the table where the Zombie kids were eating their lunch.

Oh, man. I thought. Maybe they have some cake!

But as soon as I sat down, they all got up and moved to another table.

I decided to follow them.

Every time I sat down, they got up. Kind of reminded me of the musical Zombie chairs game we play at home.

When they ran out of tables, one of the Zombie Goth kids stopped me and asked me, "Why are you following us?"

"I want to be a Zombie, like you guys," I said.

She just looked at me... Confused.

"Zombies? Look, we're just expressing our own individuality and non-conformity to the norms that society is trying to force upon us."

Now I looked at her... Confused.

"Do you have any cake?" I said.

"We're outta here." And they all got up and left the lunch room.

I guess they didn't like cake.

Man, being a kid in middle school is really confusing.

Thursday

I only had two classes today, so I thought getting through school should be pretty easy.

Today I had Warrior Class and Human Gym Class.

Warrior Class was pretty easy, because they needed stand ins for the Zombies that the warriors had to battle.

So I volunteered and pretended to be a Zombie for the whole class.

The kids gave me a lot of high fives, because they said I was really realistic.

The teacher looked at me with a weird, worried look on his face for some reason, though.

31

After lunch, we had Human Gym Class.

It was a lot like Mob Gym Class.

They had a gym teacher, a court, and they played Dodge Ball.

The only difference was that the gym teacher here had a lot of extra meat on him... especially around his mid-section.

After gym class, they said we had to go the LOKKER ROOM, to get cleaned up.

32

It was the most horrifying place I had ever been.

Seeing so many human kids without their clothes on really creeped me out.

I just wasn't used to seeing so much flesh, without it being rotten.

What really creeped me out was when they started twirling their towels and snapping them at each other.

All the kids started turning bright red, and swelling up like balloons.

Woooooooh. So disturbing.

At the end of Human Gym class, I was so happy because I finally made it through one full day of school.

I ran into Alex as I was walking home.

"You're not the real Steve, are you?" she said.

"What do you mean? He, he… Of course I'm Steve. Steve the warrior!"

"Nope. You're a Zombie, and you switched bodies with Steve, and you're just acting like him for a few weeks until the full moon, so you can visit the Swamp Witch, and she can turn you back," she said.

"Wha… How did you know?"

"Steve called me and told me," she said. "He thought you might need a friend to show you the ropes on how to fit in around here."

Good Ole' Steve, I thought.

"Plus, I could tell you weren't Steve. Steve is one of the coolest kids at school. You act like it's your first day in middle school," she said.

What! Steve is one the coolest kids at school? He never told me that.

Man, I can only imagine what kind of trouble he's getting me into at my mob school.

Friday

Oh, man! I just remembered that my ghoulfriend Sally gets back from Spring break this Sunday!

I've been so preoccupied with fitting in at human school that I forgot about her.

What am I going to tell her? Should I tell her the truth, that Steve and I switched bodies? What if it scares her away?

And, what am I going to say when I see her? "Hi, Sally. My name is Steve. I'm your new human boyfriend. And I'm a warrior, and one of the coolest kids at my school."

Who knows, maybe she might like me more.

Anyway, today at school, they announced that they were going to have a PVP Hunger Games Death Match Tournament in a few weeks.

PVP Death Match! What's that?!!

I asked one of the kids in class what it was.

"It's when all of the kids at school play each other in a game to the death. Kinda like Hunger Games but in middle school," he said.

Hunger Games? Battle to the death? Man, what did I get myself into?

"Yeah, all of the kids at school are talking about it. It's the biggest event of the year," he said.

Man, he talks about it like if he's going to a party to beat piñatas or something.

Wow, human kids are so weird.

Saturday

Today, I went to go meet Steve at our usual place, but he wasn't there.

Alex came instead.

"Hey Zombie," she said. "Steve said he was sorry he couldn't make it, but he went on a camping trip with your Mom, Dad and little brother to the Swamp Biome. He sounded really excited too. Steve really loves camping."

Oh brother, I thought. Now my family is going to totally love Steve.

"Yeah, Steve told me that he's having a really great time being a Zombie. He said he's made a ton of Mob friends, and the Principal of your school even made him the president of the Event Committee at school."

"Wha...?!!!"

"I think it's because he convinced them to have a big Dance Party in a few weeks. They really liked that idea."

Mobs dancing? I didn't even know that mobs knew how to dance. I know I can't.

"Steve wanted me to give you a message, too," she paused for a long minute. "He said, your friend Sally was attacked by a Snow Golem. He said when they found her, all that was left of her were her tonsils."

"What?!!!!"

"Naw, just kidding. Steve said Sally's not coming home for a few more weeks because she and her family got snowed in at the Snow Biome."

"Wow. That's just cold," I said.

Since I couldn't ask Steve about the PVP tournament, I decided to ask Alex about it.

"Alex, I was going to ask Steve about the PVP Hunger Games Death Match Tournament. What in the world is that?"

"Oh, that. Yeah, that's a tournament where all the kids at school fight to the death. We have it every year," she said.

"Huh?!!"

"Yeah, we start out with the entire group of kids at school, from 6th grade to 8th grade. Then we start killing each other off one by one. The person who survives is the winner," she said.

"What?!!"

"Yeah, it's a lot of fun. I can't wait for it to be here in a few weeks," she said.

I couldn't believe my new ears. These kids are just going to pick each other off, one by one, and she says it's fun?

Man, I need to be careful around these humans.

I thought about asking Alex what kind of attendance problems they have at school after the tournament, but I didn't want to cause any trouble.

Wow, human middle school is serious hostile territory.

Sunday

I finally got a chance to talk to Steve, after he got back from camping with my family.

But I was still feeling weird that my Mom and Dad asked him to go on a camping trip to the Swamp Biome.

"How was your camping trip?" I asked Steve sarcastically.

"Whoa, what's gotten under your skin?"

"Nothing! I'm human now, remember!" I shouted.

"Zombie, what's bothering you?" Steve asked.

"I'm just mad that all of a sudden my Mom and Dad, my little brother, all my friends, and everyone at school thinks you're awesome,

41

while I'm having such a hard time trying to fit in with all these crazy kids at school!"

"Actually, everybody at your mob school thinks YOU'RE awesome," Steve said.

"Oh… Yeah… That's right." I thought about what Steve just said.

"But how did you get them to like you so quick? I was a Zombie for twelve years and I couldn't even get the neighbor's cat to like me."

"I think it's because I didn't try to get them to like me. I just tried to really get to know them. As I got to know them better, it was easy to find something that we had in common," he said with a shrug.

"Oh…"

"And the kids in my middle school are just scared little kids who really want everyone else to like them," he said. "I actually feel sorry for them sometimes."

"Really?"

"Yeah. I think what most kids in school are looking for is a friend that will like them no matter what," he said. "So, I try to be a friend like that to everybody at school. After doing it for a while, I ended up with a lot of friends."

"Wow, I feel like a real dummy."

"Don't worry about it. Next time, just don't beat your brains out trying to figure it out," Steve said.

Wow, I thought only Zombies did that.

"Thanks, Steve," I said.

"Anytime, bro…" he said as he hobbled away.

Monday

Today I found a box under Steve's bed.

It looked like he was trying to hide it from the villagers he lived with.

It was really far back under the bed, but I was finally able to pull it out.

When I got it out and opened it, it was full of magazines.

But, these were the weirdest magazines I had ever seen.

The magazines were about magical ponies that liked to sing and dance.

The ponies were the best of friends, and
as long as they were friends, they could
overcome anything.

I'm kinda weirded out that Steve has these.

I've got to ask him about them when I see
him next time.

Tuesday

Today, one of the villagers I live with said that my breath was really bad.

I told him how happy I was for him to say that.

He just looked at me… Confused.

Then I remembered how everything in Steve's world was different from my world.

So I went to my room to brush my teeth.

I've only used a toothbrush once, when I wanted to get back at my Mom for making me dirty my room.

But man, this time I had to brush ten times as many teeth!

By the time I finished, I was exhausted.

I had fun picking my nose and getting all of the boogers out, though.

I think noses are awesome, especially the hairy things that grow out of them.

I like them because it's easier to reach the boogers that get stuck in there.

Zombies normally have to dig real deep to get boogers out, and it's a lot of work.

Kinda like mining for diamonds.

I tried to start a booger collection here, like the one I have at home.

But I think the villagers thought it was gross and threw them away.

I was really bummed too. Those come in real handy when I need a midnight snack.

I'm still having a hard time with the SHA-WUR, though.

I just can't figure out what to do when I'm in there.

It's really weird being wet. Zombies aren't supposed to get wet.

It's also really weird having to walk around in wet clothes all day.

I went downstairs and the villagers were eating the weirdest food.

I think they called it OLD-MEAL.

Kinda grossed me out because it reminded me of brains.

"What do you want for lunch today, Steve?" The villager lady asked me.

"Do you have any spider eyes and cake? They're my favorite!" I said.

The villager lady just looked at me... Confused.

Then she showed me what she made for me for lunch.

It was in a weird container that was separated in sections. I think she called it a BEN-TOE lunch.

Kind of weird since it didn't have any toes in it.

"Looks kind of weird. Can I fix it up a bit?" I asked.

"Sure," she said.

Then I rearranged everything so that it would look a bit more edible.

"Now that's better!" I said.

The villager lady just looked at me…
Confused.

Wednesday

Today I had a class that was supposed to teach you everything about mining.

I always wanted to know what Steve does all day in these caves.

As a Zombie, I like going into the caves to go exploring, bother some cave spiders, or even ride some minecarts.

But all these humans ever do is bang at the wall with a funny tool called a pickaxe.

And all they talk about is, DIAMONDS, DIAMONDS, DIAMONDS.

I did learn a few things in Mining class, though.

I learned why some people mine at night.

The teacher said that some people mine at night so they can have a better chance at finding diamonds, and so that they can keep all the diamonds to themselves.

"Why don't they just share their diamonds with everyone else?" I asked the teacher. "There's plenty of diamonds in the caves to go around."

The teacher just looked at me… Confused.

For some reason, people keep looking at me with that confused look on their faces. Maybe that's just one of the weird things about being human.

It's really starting to creep me out, though.

In the middle of Mining class, we heard a sound.

"Uuuurrrggghhh!"

"Quick, everyone! Get out of the caves! There's a Zombie coming!" the teacher said.

After everyone left, I stuck around to see who it was.

"Uuuurrrggghhh!"

"Steve!"

"Hey, Zombie. Whatcha up to? Uuuurrrrggghhhh!"

"I was just in Mining class when you came by," I said.

"Yeah, that class is really boring," he said. "You know, I can't understand why people don't just share all the diamonds they find with everyone else."

"So what are you doing here?" I said.

"I really love scaring villagers and miners and stuff," he said. "I like seeing the look on their faces, and they usually drop really cool stuff. The other day, some lady dropped a whole cake. It was the best day ever!"

"You seem to be liking Zombie life a lot," I said.

"Being a Zombie is like the most fun I've had in a long time!" Steve said.

"I don't have to take a bath; I don't have to brush my teeth; I can pick my nose and eat my boogers without anyone calling me gross, and I can leave my room as dirty as I want it."

Wow. I never thought I had it so good.

"So when are we going to switch back?" he asked.

"Wha..? You still want to switch back? I thought you were having fun?"

"Yeah, it's fun and all. But it's like going on vacation. It's fun to take a break and do something fun, but eventually you've got to go home and get back to work," he said.

Wow. Steve is so deep. No wonder everybody likes him.

"Well, the Swamp Witch doesn't appear for a few more weeks. So we need to keep acting like each other until then," I said.

All of a sudden, we heard the Mining class teacher and the class coming our way.

"Well, I'll see you later, bro," Steve said as he disappeared into the caves.

Wow. I guess being a Zombie isn't so bad after all.

Thursday

After class, me and Alex met by the lake so she could help me practice being more human.

"So, Zombie, I want you to repeat after me," she said.

"Hi, my name is Steve." And then she stuck her hand out.

"Hi, my name is Steve," I said, and I stuck my hand out.

"No, Zombie, use the other hand," she said.

"No, Zombie, use the other hand," I said.

"No, No, just the hand," she said.

"No, No, just the hand," I said.

"Uuuurrrgghhh!" she yelled.

"That's one's easy!" I said. "Uuuurrrgghhh!"

I don't know why, but she started turning red. Maybe it was something she ate.

"Let's try something different," she said. "Where are you from?"

"You know that's a great question," I said. "I've been asking my Mom that question for a long time now, and she doesn't seem to give me a straight answer. My friend Skelee thinks Zombies come from eggs, but I…"

"No, No, No. You're supposed to be Steve, remember?"

"Oh yeah. Sorry. But wait a minute. Where is Steve from, anyway? He said he just appeared one day in a villager's bed."

Alex, just looked at me… Confused.

Again, with the confused look! I just thought, if a fly passes by her face, her face is going to get stuck like that forever.

Well, we practiced all afternoon until the sun started setting.

As I walked home, all I could think about was where Steve actually came from.

It must be really hard not knowing who your parents are, or where you came from, I thought.

Man, I really miss my Mom and Dad right now.

I even miss my little brat brother.

I hope me and Steve can switch back soon.

Friday

Today I decided to try to be a friend to one of the kids at school.

But boy, it was a lot harder than I thought.

The hardest part was just getting someone to talk to me.

As soon as I walked up to them, they kept doing that eye rolling thing, and walking away.

I thought I would try to make friends with one of the kids on the FOOT-BALL team.

They were easy to find because they were really big and tall.

So I walked up to a group of them hanging out in the hallway.

"Hi, my name is Steve," I said. "What's yours?"

"My name is Nunnayorbizness," one of them said.

That's a weird name, I thought.

"So...Nunnayorbizness? How's it going?"

"Whatsitooya?" another kid said.

Wow, these kids have got some strange names.

"What grade are you in, Whatsittooya?"

"Whyyaaskin," another boy said.

Man, do all the kids in this school have weird names?

"So, are you part of any cool clubs, Whyyaaskin?"

"Whydooyoocare?" the last kid said.

Man, whatever happened to simple names like Steve?

"So…Whydooyoocare. What do you like to do for fun?"

"Nunnayorbizness," they all said. Then they walked away laughing.

Wow, making friends in middle school is really, really hard…

Saturday

Today, Alex came over so that we could keep practicing being human.

But I was still having a hard time with this "trying to fit in" thing at school.

So I thought maybe Alex could help me with it.

"Alex, I have a question for you."

"Sure. What's bugging you?" she asked.

"Nothing. I wish it was, though. I miss those bugs… But anyway, I wanted to ask you, why is it so hard to fit in at school?"

"Sounds like you're having a hard time," she said.

"Hard?!! It's impossible. Everybody is so different. And then everybody makes me feel like I don't belong anywhere. I just want to be myself, but I can't because I have to be Steve. But the harder I try to be Steve, the more I keep making the dumb mistakes I usually make."

"So the more you try to be Steve, the more you end up acting like yourself?" she said.

"Yeah… I guess."

"Maybe if you just be yourself, you'll end up being more like Steve," she said.

Wow. I thought Steve was deep. Alex is pretty deep too.

"Zombie, who you are is not who you are on the outside, it's who you are on the inside."

"You mean I'm guts, organs, and entrails?" I said, confused.

"No, Zombie. That's just your body. Who you are is what is living inside your body."

"You mean like slugs, maggots, and tapeworms?" I asked.

"No, No. Who you are is what is living in your head."

"You, know. Now that you mention it, I had an uncle that had a bird's nest in his head…" I said.

"Forget it, Zombie. One day, you'll understand."

I was going to ask her more questions, but she started turning red again.

So I went home thinking about what Alex said.

"The more you are yourself, the more you will be like Steve."

I didn't really understand what she meant about the Steve part, but I think I'm going to start being my old Zombie self from now on.

Look out Overworld! Here comes Zombie Steve!

Sunday

The villagers I live with invited me to dinner tonight with the Priest that runs the town.

They said that all of the important villagers in the town would be there.

I didn't know what that meant. But I said yes anyway.

I thought, this would be the perfect opportunity for me to be my Zombie self again.

So the first thing I did was to make sure I smelled right.

There was a pig farmer in the village, so I decided to roll around with the pigs for a little while.

One thing I love about pigs is that out of all of the different animals, they smell the closest to what Zombies smell like.

I made sure to rub some cow pies on me too, to add a bit more zest to the mix.

My breath was only a little stinky because I didn't brush my teeth this morning. So I decided to spice it up with a little help from some stinky gym socks I was saving for a rainy day.

My clothes didn't have enough holes on them, so I tore a few more.

And what really topped it off was a nice infestation of maggots in my hair, ears, and clothes.

I had a bunch left over, so I just kept the rest in my pocket for a snack later.

Aaahhh. I felt like my old self again.

I thought, "Look Out Overworld! Look Out villagers! Zombie Steve is here!"

I got lost on my way to the Priest's house. So, I tried to ask for directions. But people were just looking at me with that same confused look on their face, all over town.

I wonder if there's something in the water that's making them look like that. Too much of that can't be good for you, I thought.

So I finally found the Priest's house, and it was really, really big. I think they said that the Priest is the Mayor of the village, whatever that means. It probably just means you have a big house.

I knocked and a waiter villager answered the door. Again, he had that confused look on his face. But this time he ran away holding his mouth like he had a bug that was trying to get out or something.

That happens to Zombies whenever the tapeworms in our stomachs grow too big. When they start coming out, I like to play with them and act like I have a really long tongue.

Well, I went in, and after walking around for a few minutes, I finally found the dining room.

As soon as I walked in, I saw a bunch of villagers in different colored robes.

All of a sudden, their faces changed color. One lady turned blue. Another man turned purple. One guy turned really white. And another villager turned green.

It was really cool. I didn't know humans could change colors like that.

What was even cooler was how they made their faces match the color of their robes. What control! I thought.

I saw an empty seat so I sat down in it. It was actually the seat right next to the Priest and his wife. I pulled my hand out of my pocket to shake hands with the Priest's wife, but I forgot that I had a pocket full of maggots.

"Oops. Sorry about that. I forgot I had some extra maggots in my pocket. Does anybody want some?"

Next thing I know, everybody at the table starts puking.

What was really cool was how they puked one right after the other, all around the table. It reminded me of the Zombie wave we used to do when my dad would take me to Zombie baseball games.

Now it started to feel like home.

The villagers I live with were running a little late. So when they got there, all of the other villagers were either sleeping on the table, under the table, or on the floor.

I was just having fun making vomit angels on the floor, like I do at home with my Mom and Dad. There wasn't the usual amount of vomit that we have when we play at home, but it was still cool.

The villagers' eyes got real big and their mouths were hanging open.

Then they started making a funny noise... "HURRRRR, HURRRRR, HURRRRR" was all they would say.

"HURRRRR, HURRRRR, HURRRRR" was all they said on the way home, too.

I guess they must have been really sad that they missed all the fun.

I thought it was a really nice dinner, if you ask me.

Alex called me later and asked what happened. She said that half of the town was hysterical because of what happened at the Mayor's house.

I told her that I took her advice and that I was going to "be myself so I could be more like Steve." And it worked out great!

All I heard on the other side of the phone was the sound, "Doh!"

"Hey, Zombie…" she said.

"Yeah, Alex?"

"Never mind…" she said as she closed the phone.

Wow, I'm finally starting to fit in around here.

Sweet.

Monday

I woke up this morning, and there was a bucket full of stuff next to my bed.

On the side of the bucket was a big sign that said, "USE ME, PLEASE!!!"

Inside the bucket was a bunch of stuff I had never seen before.

There was a bottle of something called SHAM-POO. It said you're supposed to put it on your hair.

And I thought only Zombies put poo in their hair. Cool.

There was a really big toothbrush in the bucket. It was so big, I thought the person who uses this thing must have teeth as big as my head.

There was a sign on it that said it was something called a SCRUB-BRUSH.

Then there was a tube of something called TOOF-PAYST, which said it goes with something called MOUF-WASH.

There was also a bottle of something called LO-SHIN that looked kinda creamy like Mushroom stew.

And there was a big bar of SO-AP, which I've already seen before.

Inside the bucket were instructions on how to use everything.

I thought I would read the instructions while I got in the SHA-WUR, to save time.

But then the paper melted!

Man, what was I supposed to do with all this stuff now?

75

I tried calling Alex, but for some reason the phone stopped working.

I thought maybe I pressed the wrong button. But, it was hard to read the numbers with all that water spraying all over the place.

I guess I have to figure it out by myself, I thought.

So, I got out of the SHA-WUR, and grabbed the bottle of SHAM-POO.

I poured the whole bottle on my head.

I didn't think it smelled like poo at all.

But, I finally realized why it's so much better to be a Zombie, and not have eyes.

Then I grabbed the brush and I put the TOOF-PAYST on it.

But I had the hardest time trying to fit the brush in my mouth.

I think this brush was made for somebody like Mutant.

So I kept pushing until I finally got it in my mouth.

I had a really hard time moving it around though.

I grabbed the bottle of MOUF-WASH and used the whole thing.

Good thing I had it too. I was really thirsty.

The bottle of LO-SHIN said I needed to use it on my hands and my face.

So I opened it up and poured it all over my face. Kind of felt like the vomit baths Mom used to give me when I was a kid. But it didn't smell as good.

I didn't know what to do with the bucket, so I just put it on my head like I saw some other Zombies do back home.

I was actually pretty proud of myself.

And, I was really excited to show the villagers how good I looked.

When I came downstairs, all the villagers dropped what they were doing.

Then they started making that funny noise again.

"HUURRRRRRR...HUURRRRRRRR..."

I wonder if that sound means that they're really happy.

Cool.

I ran into Alex on my way to school, and she just looked at me... Confused.

She took me by the hand and led me all the way to the back of the school.

79

She took the bucket off of my head and walked over to where there was a large hose.

All of a sudden water came out of the hose and hit me right in the face.

"HEEEEYYYYYY!!! Why'd you do that?" I yelled as I stood there soaking wet.

"Trust me. It was for your own good," she said.

After, she dried me with a bunch of paper towels.

"Wow, you smell really nice," she said.

I didn't think so…

Tuesday

Today, I realized that if I didn't want to get killed during the PVP Hunger Games Death Match Tournament, then I needed to get ready.

So, I decided to do some Tree Punching exercises.

Hey, if Steve can punch a tree, so can I.

I found a tree nearby that was nice and thick and strong.

I was trying to remember what Steve did when he punched trees.

I always thought it was the weirdest thing to punch trees. But I would always catch Steve doing it.

I just couldn't understand how he did it without losing any fingers or anything.

Well, here it goes…

WHAAAMMM!

"YYYEEEEEOOOOWWW!!!!!!"

Man, that hurt!

I must've done it wrong. Because it hurt like crazy.

Maybe I hit it with the wrong hand. Let me try again...

WHAAAMMM!

"YYYEEEEEOOOOWWW!!!!!!"

Uuuurrrgghhh! Why is this not working?!!!

Maybe this is just a dumb tree! I bet if I kicked it, it'll break...

WHAAAMMM!

"YYYEEEEEOOOOWWW!!!!!!"

Uuuuurrrgghhh! Oh Man, I think I broke my foot!

This reminded me of when I took my Zombie Karate test.

What did the teacher say again? "Good work using your head?"

83

Well, what have I got to lose?

WHAAAMMM!

POP!

Hey! I did it! A tree block just popped out of the tree!

Well, I may not be able to punch a tree with my hand, or kick it with my foot…

But when the time comes, I can always beat my head against a tree until I figure it out.

But, ooooohhh, my head really hurts…

Wednesday

Today I had a class that was supposed to teach you how to survive during a Zombie Apocalypse.

It was taught by Master Sergeant Fuller B. Loney again.

Man, I hope I can keep it together for this class, I thought.

"Zombies are dumb, ugly and walk real slow, which puts you at an advantage," he said. "And as long as you follow the rules I give you, not only can you survive a Zombie Apocalypse, but you can also keep a Zombie as a pet if you want to."

What?!!!

"Rule number 1… Build a strong shelter where you can go to for the night."

Man, that won't work, I thought. Zombies can bang down doors you know. Duh!

"Rule number 2… Make sure you gather enough food for the night."

Yeah, cause if you don't we're going to get you! He, he…

"Rule number 3… Make weapons that allow you to kill Zombies with the least amount of strikes, like an enchanted sword or enchanted bow and arrow."

Huh… You can do that?

"Rule number 4… Block Zombies from getting into your shelter by using fences, slabs, and carpets. You can get out, but they can't get in."

Are you serious?

"Rule number 5… Try to trick Zombies into going into water."

Yeah, like that's going to happen…

"Rule number 6… Set up traps around your shelter that will completely annihilate any Zombies. You can use fire, lava, cactus, TNT, and sand blocks dropping on their head."

Man, these guys are serious!

"Rule number 7… Zombies hate wolves, so get yourself a pack of pet wolves to protect you and your shelter."

I thought Mom said I was just allergic to those things. Weird.

"Rule number 8… Try to lure a Zombie next to the edge of a cliff. Knock the Zombie off with one blow of your sword, bow and arrow, or even your hand."

OMG!

"Rule number 9... Try to knock a creeper into a group of Zombies to do optimal damage. If you can knock a charged creeper into them, even better. You can put on the dropped Zombie heads as camouflage, or just use it as a cool trophy to hang on your wall."

I think I'm gonna be sick.

"Rule number 10... Keep the Zombies occupied as long as possible until sunrise. Then they'll catch on fire and you can use their rotten flesh as a quick breakfast."

BBBLLLEEEEECCCHHH!!!!!! Splat!

So much for keeping it together...

Thursday

Today, I decided to make friends with one of the kids that seem to hang out by themselves all of the time.

I chose a little fat kid, because I knew he couldn't run too fast.

Also, because he kinda reminded me of Slimey back home.

"Why are you talking to me?!!" he said.

"You look like you can use a friend," I said.

"How did you know?" he asked.

"Oh, just a guess…"

"My name is Steve, by the way," I said.

"I know you who you are. You're one of the cool kids in school. But I shouldn't be talking to you."

"What do you mean?"

"The cool kids don't usually hang out with kids like me," he said.

"Why not?"

"I don't know." He shrugged. "They just don't."

"Then how do you know we won't get along?" I said.

He just stood there... Confused.

"Well, I won't tell, if you won't," I said.

He smiled.

"What's your name, anyway?"

"My name is Eli."

"It's good to meet you, Eli."

"It's good to meet you too, Steve."

"Hey, Eli. Can I ask you something?"

"Sure."

"Do you have any cake?"

Eli just looked at me, again… Confused.

Wow, I made a new friend today! And I did it all by myself.

Eli told me that he lived really close to Steve's house, too. Actually, he told me he was Steve's neighbor.

That's so cool.

But I was just really happy I made a friend.

Friday

Today, I planned to meet Alex after school so I could tell her the good news that I made a friend yesterday.

She told me to meet her on the mountain, behind the school. She said it had a great view.

So, after school, I followed the trail up the mountain to meet Alex.

I got there early and I took a peek over the edge of the mountain to see how high it was.

Whew! This is really, really high. I would hate to fall down that thing, I thought.

I tried to lean over the mountain to see if I could see the bottom.

All of a sudden Alex surprised me. "Hey Zombie!"

It was such a surprise that I fell over the mountain!

AAAAAAAAAAAHHHHHH!!!! I yelled all the way down…

Saturday

I woke up this morning, in my bed, at the villagers' house.

I came downstairs and Alex was having breakfast with the villagers.

"Hey Steve. Did you sleep well?" Alex asked, as she pointed with her finger to meet her outside.

"Yeah, I did," I said. "But I had the weirdest nightmare that I fell off a mountain."

The villagers just looked at me... Confused.

I walked outside to meet Alex.

"That wasn't a dream, Zombie," she said. "You really did fall off the mountain."

"What? Then how come I'm still in one piece?"

"Steve didn't tell you?" she asked, surprised.

"Tell me what?"

"Well, whenever Steve dies, he just reappears in his bed in the villager's house."

"Are you serious?"

"Yeah. He dies all the time. And bam! He just appears in his bed."

"Can you do it?" I asked Alex.

"Sure can. Except I try not to do it too much. I mean, it takes so much work trying to collect all my stuff again."

"What do you mean?" I asked.

"Well, when you die, you leave all your stuff," she said. "Then you've got to retrace your steps to go find your stuff again. And if you don't get there quick enough, somebody else takes your stuff."

Wow. This is awesome. So I can die, and then just appear in my bed? This is a dream come true!

"Hey, I want to try dying," I said.

"Really? Now?"

"Yeah, let's do it right now. Maybe you can hit me over the head. Or you can throw me off a cliff again. Or you can…"

Next thing, I hear, "Thwip!"

"That'll work too," I said as I clutched at the arrow in my head.

Next thing I know, I'm waking up in my bed.

"HA! This is awesome!"

I ran downstairs, past the villagers and the confused looks on their faces, and outside to see Alex.

"That's a really cool trick!" I could hardly believe it worked.

"Yeah. It really comes in handy during our Death Match PVP tournaments," she said. "Which reminds me, we need to start practicing for that. It's coming up real soon."

"Oooohhh! Now I get it. Death Match, because if anyone dies, they wake up in their bed…Oooohhh!"

"Yeah, well, it's coming up soon, and we want to make sure we win," Alex said.

"What do you win?"

"You win the right to be the King of the Mountain," she said. "Which usually means you get a lot of respect at school. Me and

Steve have won it for the past two years, and this year we're going to make it three."

Wow. Alex is intense, I thought. Kind of a little too intense for me.

"So get some rest," Alex said. "Tomorrow we start training."

Sunday

Alex came to my house bright and early this morning.

I'm actually starting to like the daytime. Just not the morning. I like sleeping in.

"Wake up, sleepy head," Alex said. "It's time to start training."

I got up and met her outside.

"Come on!"

"Where are you taking me?"

"I'm taking you on the road to victory," she said with a creepy look on her face.

When we got to the other side of the mountain, I could not believe my eyes...

"Whoa..."

Alex had set up the biggest obstacle course I have ever seen.

"When did you set this up?" I asked her.

"I did it all last night while you were sleeping. This is the rig me and Steve practice on. We call it... The Gauntlet!"

"Whoa..."

"I'm going to teach you all of the secret moves me and Steve use to win the PVP Hunger Games Death Match Tournament," Alex said.

"Gulp…" was all I could say.

"So, are you ready?"

"Ready…" I squeaked out.

"Well, first thing you need to know is that your best weapons are your bow, sword, and flint and steel," she said. "You want to get your opponents before they even come close to you. With a bow you can shoot them from far away. With the flint and steel, you can set them on fire as they chase you. Then you can use your sword to finish them off."

"Whoa…"

"Make sure you have a golden apple or some cake to replenish your energy," she said.

"But most important of all… Are you paying attention?"

I guess she didn't like me picking my nose and eating boogers while she was talking.

"The most important tip of all…The mother of all tips…The one thing that will make sure that you dominate the PVP Hunger Games Death Match every time is…"

RIIINNNGGG!

"Hold on, Zombie, my Mom is calling," she said to me before answering.

I just stood there looking at the enormous Gauntlet thing that was standing in front of me.

What have I gotten myself into? I bet I'm going to get killed like the first minute this PVP thing starts.

Maybe I should just get killed on purpose, that way I'll just be in my bed and wait until it's all over.

But man, if I do that, Alex will be by herself. And I know Steve would never ditch her like that.

Also, if we don't win, that means I would've ruined Steve's social life.

Wow, talk about pressure.

"Zombie, I'm sorry, but I've got to go. he baby sitter can't make it so my Mom says I have to go home and watch my little brother."

"Sure…" At this point, I'm not even listening to her. 'm just thinking about the epic fail this whole tournament is going to be.

"Don't worry, Zombie. We got this. You'll do great."

I try to smile as she walked away, but all I could do is give a smirk.

Then I realized, I probably have that confused look on my face, don't I?

Monday

Today all the kids at school were talking about the upcoming PVP Hunger Games Death Match Tournament.

They even had posters all around the school to remind everybody.

I heard some kids talking about how everybody is picking teams to be a part of.

They said that you survive longer if you are part of a team.

And if you're not part of a team, then you usually get killed within the first few minutes of the game.

Wow, I'm glad I'm with Alex, I thought.

I ran into Eli at school, and I asked him if he was part of any teams.

"Naw, kids like me usually get killed in the first few minutes of the game," he said. "But, I sure wish that I could be on a winning team for once."

"Why don't you join my team?" I asked Eli.

Eli was really psyched about that idea.

So was I.

Alex, not so much...

Tuesday

Me and Eli met Alex after school to start our training.

Alex pulled me to the side and started telling how really mad she was at me for inviting Eli to be part of our team.

"Zombie, how are we going to win if we have to drag Eli with us everywhere?" she said.

"Well, he's never been part of a winning team, and I thought it would be great for him to feel like a winner for once," I said.

I think Alex understood that I wasn't just talking about Eli. But it would be a win for all of the kids in school that feel like losers.

"I guess it's alright." She sighed. "But this means that we have to train even harder."

"Sure," I said with hesitation.

"I'm just glad we have our secret weapon."

"What's the secret weapon?" asked.

"I'll tell you later," she said. "First we need to focus on training. Remember, first we walk, then we run…"

The only thing I was thinking about running from is this PVP Tournament, I thought.

"Alex, I heard the kids at school talking about getting together in teams," I said. "But, I thought there is only one winner at the end of the game."

"Yeah, what they do is get together in teams to defeat all of the other players. Once they do that, then they either turn on each other, or they sacrifice themselves and let one of their teammates win."

"Whoa."

"And, we're up against some tough teams this year, too," she said. "The two toughest teams are the Jocks, who are the strongest, and the Nerds who are the smartest. All the rest of the teams get annihilated in the first day of the Tournament. By the second day, there are only two teams left. Hopefully it will be us, and one of those other teams."

"And that's when we use our secret weapon," she added.

"What secret weapon?!!" I said frantically.

"You'll see," she said… "You'll see."

Wednesday

Eli and I met with Alex after school again today so that we could train for the PVP Tournament.

She made us run through the Gauntlet over and over and over.

It was really tough.

But I really felt bad for Eli. I don't think he's ever run a day in his life.

Alex was turning really red. Redder than I've ever seen her before.

Whatever she ate must be really messing with her now.

I noticed she turned the most red when Eli ran the Gauntlet.

Maybe being around little fat kids makes her queasy.

Well, we stopped training when the sun started setting.

I walked Eli home. Actually, I carried him home because he couldn't really walk anymore.

When I got home I called Steve to see what he was up to.

"I'm just practicing my dance moves for the big Dance Party this Saturday," he said.

"Are you guys really going to have a dance party?" I asked.

"We sure are," he said. "All the guys are getting ready too. I taught them some moves that I think will make them really shine."

Whoa.

"Yeah. Skelee is going to do the Robot, and Slimey is practicing his Square Dancing," he said.

"What about Creepy?" I asked.

"I think Creepy said he's gonna do some break dancing," Steve said.

I don't know how I felt about that.

"Hey, Steve. I found out that the full moon is on Saturday," I said. "So we need to be in the middle of the Swamp Biome by then. Then we can find the Swamp Witch so she can turn us back to normal."

"Yeah, I can head out after the Dance Party and meet you over there," Steve said.

"Sounds great," I said.

"How's it going preparing for the PVP Tournament?" Steve asked.

"It's going great! We just picked up another teammate. His name is Eli. He's actually your neighbor."

"You mean the little fat kid that lives next door? Doesn't he always get killed in the first few minutes of the tournament?"

"Yeah, but he's really determined to win this year."

"OK, cool. Don't forget to use our secret weapon for winning the tournament," he said.

"What secret weapon?"

"Oh, it's really good," Steve said. "It's what really helped us dominate all of the other teams the past few years. As long as you use the secret weapon, you can't lose."

"Well, what is it?!!!"

"Out of all the things you do, no matter what the situation, and no matter who you're up against, you just have to, absolutely, make sure you—"

Click.

Oh man, my phone died! Uuuurrrgghhh! Why does this keep happening?!!

Man, the same thing happened to me when I was in the SHA-WUR this morning!

I just have to make sure that the first thing I do tomorrow is ask Alex about the secret weapon.

Otherwise we're dead.

Thursday

I didn't see Alex at school all day.

Me and Eli met up at the Gauntlet after
school, but Alex wasn't there either.

I tried calling her on my cellphone, but for
some reason she didn't answer.

But, then I noticed that I had a message on
my phone.

I played it back, and it was Alex leaving me a
message.

I put it on speaker so that me and Eli could
hear it together.

"Hey Zombie, it's me Alex.

Well, I've got some bad news. It seems that my little brother caught the chicken pox, and now I have it too.

My Mom took me to the Doctor, and after checking me, he told my Mom that I have to stay out of school for the next few weeks. The Doctor says that I'm contagious and doesn't want me to give it to everybody at school.

So, I'm really sorry, but this means I'm going to have to miss the PVP Tournament.

But don't worry. Just remember what I'm about to tell you, and you and Eli will do just fine.

The single, most important thing you need to remember to win the tournament, no matter what situation you are in, and no matter who you're up against—the most important thing you need to do is…"

Click.

Uuuurrrggghhh! It happened again! This phone is such a pain!

"Eli, can I use your phone to call Alex?"

"I don't have a cellphone," he said.

Oh, man. Now we have no way of calling Alex or Steve, and the Tournament is tomorrow!

"So, what are we going to do?" Eli asked.

"I don't know, Eli..."

At that moment I had to decide if I was going to quit, and let Steve, Alex and Eli down, or if I was going to stick it out and fight.

All I knew was that whatever I decided, it was going to determine the kind of person, Zombie or human, that I was going to be for the rest of my middle school life.

Man, this is just too much pressure for a twelve year old Zombie to handle.

Friday

Well, today I'm either going to have a big victory, or I'm going to wake up in my bed in utter shame.

I tried calling Eli in the morning to give him a pep talk, but my cellphone was totally dead.

Eli told me it was probably all of those calls that I made while I was in the SHA-WUR.

I just think Steve gave me a really bad phone.

So I finished getting ready and went to school to face my destiny.

At school they picked us in up in buses and took us to the field where we were going to have the tournament.

This is my last journal entry…unless I make it back from the battle field.

Will I make it till tomorrow? I don't know.

But I decided that I would give it my best. If not for me, then for Steve and Alex and my new friend Eli.

And whether I win or lose, live or die, I will at least know that I was courageous enough to face whatever challenges my twelve year old life dished out to me.

Bring it!

Friday Night Entry

I can't believe we survived the first day of the tournament!

I was sure that we would be annihilated in the first few minutes.

But there we were, with all of the other kids, waiting for the horn to blow.

Once it did, me and Eli ran as hard as we could to the first chest of items.

Lucky for us, there was a sword and a bow and arrow inside.

So, instead of collecting items, we just attacked every person that we saw.

Which was kind of hard because our eyes were closed most of the time.

Before I knew it, we collected so many supplies from the people we attacked that we had all of the supplies we needed to last throughout the game.

The Jocks were fiercely annihilating most of the other teams.

The Nerds were blowing up all of the main people they thought would be important in helping the other teams to win. Without leaders, all of the other kids scattered, which made it easy to pick them off.

Then Eli came up with the best idea ever.

"Hey Steve," he said. "Since we have so many supplies, why don't we just hide out until all of the other teams destroy each other? Then we can just come out and be ready for tomorrow."

It was the smartest thing I ever heard.

So me and Eli just camped out on top of a really tall tree, and we just waited till all of the other teams destroyed each other.

Every now and then someone would try to climb our tree, but Eli would just shoot them down with his bow and arrow.

At the end of the night, they announced all of the people that were left in the tournament. And the only ones left were me and Eli and two of the members of the Jock's team.

We did it!

Now all we have to do is to get through tomorrow. Gulp.

Saturday Morning

I don't know how we did it, but we made it through to today.

Eli asked me a really strange question last night, and I was thinking about it all night.

"Hey Steve," he said. "If we're the last ones, doesn't that mean one of us has to die if the other person is going to win?"

"I guess so," I said. "I just never expected us to make it this far."

"Yeah. I guess so too," he said.

If we do win, I thought, I'm probably going to let Eli win. I know that's what Steve would do.

Alex, not so much…

123

So, we're going to climb down the tree now.

Who knows what's waiting for us down there.

But no matter what happens, at least I'll have a really good story to tell all my friends back home.

Saturday Night

Here I am, lying in my bed, just thinking about all that happened today.

I still can't believe the way things turned out.

Who would've thought that after getting down from that tree that things could've gone the way they did?

It's almost like the Jocks knew what we were going to do before we did it.

They were just waiting for us at the bottom of that tree, ready to attack us and send us to our comfortable beds, while they enjoyed their sweet victory.

But I don't think they were ready for what Eli was going to do.

That small, chubby kid made me so proud.

I mean, I don't know what came over him. But all of a sudden he became a PVP Hunger Games Death Match Tournament Master.

With just one shot, he was able to bounce his arrow off a tree and hit one of the Jocks hiding behind a tree. That caused that Jock to shoot his bow and arrow at a rock, and it bounced off to hit the other Jock hiding behind a bush.

The weirdest part was that Eli did it with his eyes closed…

Man, he must have a sixth sense or something.

So there we were. Just me and Eli. Celebrating our victory.

But then it hit us… Only one of us could go home with the trophy.

I knew that it was time for me to really show how much I appreciated my short, chubby friend.

Plus, this was Eli's moment to shine, not mine.

So, I told Eli to pick up his bow and arrow and win this tournament for the both of us.

Eli, was so happy. But, he was sad at the same time.

He raised his bow and arrow and aimed it at me.

I closed my eyes, and waited to wake up in my bed at the villagers' house.

But, it was kind of weird when nothing happened.

I opened one eye to peek at what was going on. Eli was standing there with his bow and arrow pulled back, aiming at me, but with his eyes closed.

Then, all of a sudden, he pointed the bow and arrow into the sky and shot.

The arrow bounced off a tree again, then bounced off a rock, and then bounced off another tree and hit him instead!

As I think about it now, I realize that Eli taught me something really important today.

He taught me what the real, true meaning of friendship is.

He taught me that it doesn't matter how you look, or what you say or what you do. But, what really matters is that you care.

And Eli cared more than anyone I have ever met.

I'm gonna miss that kid.

But, then I remembered that I had to meet Steve at the Swamp Biome.

Since the Swamp Biome is closer to my village, I picked up the bow and arrow and shot at a tree like Eli did.

Next thing I know, I'm in my bed.

And now, I need to go talk to a witch about getting my twelve year old Zombie life back…

Really Late Saturday Night Entry

I made it to the Swamp Biome and I found Steve sitting outside of the Witch's hut.

Skelee, Slimey, and Creepy were all there too.

"Hey fellas!"

"Zombie!!!" they yelled.

"Man, it's good to see you," Skelee said.

"What was it like living with the humans?" Slimey asked.

"Is it true they teach you to knock creepers into Zombies to blow them up?" Creepy asked.

"It's great to see you guys too. But right now, me and Steve need to go talk to a witch," I said.

"Hey Steve, we need to watch out for this witch. I forgot to tell you that she has a craving for rotten flesh."

"Don't worry about me," he said. "If she wants rotten flesh, I'll give her something to chew on." He shook his fist.

Me and Steve look at each other and give each other a nod that we were ready.

We knock on the door of the witch's house, ready for whatever was going to come out of that door.

"I'll be there in one minute," she answered in a really weird voice.

Then she opened the door.

Me and Steve were blown away.

She didn't look like any of the other witches I've ever seen before.

"Hello, come in, I've been expecting you," she said.

"You have?" me and Steve say together.

"Yes, after your talk with the witch in your neighborhood, she gave me a call and told me you would be coming. I prepared a potion that can turn Steve into a human again."

"But aren't you supposed to crave rotten flesh or something?" I said.

"Oh, no. Those are just stories the other witches say about me," she said. "They're all so jealous."

"What about Zombie?" Steve asked. "Can you turn him back into a Zombie?"

"Unfortunately, there is no potion for that," the witch said.

Steve and I both looked at each other, really sad.

"There's no potion for that, because all you have to do to turn a human into a Zombie is to bite them," she added. "Don't you boys ever watch the movies?"

"That's it?!!" I said, not believing what I just heard. "We could've done that weeks ago."

Then while I'm talking, Steve takes my hand and bites it.

All of a sudden, I start feeling queasy and dizzy and the whole room starts to spin.

I fall to the ground and start to shake.

Then after a while, my head hits the ground and everything goes black.

Next thing I know, Steve and the other guys are slapping me in the face to wake me up.

"OW! That hurts!" I said. "Hey, did it work?"

"Look in the mirror," Steve said.

I look in the mirror, and there I am…a
Zombie again!

I'm so happy I start jumping up and down.

Then my body parts start to fall off again,
just like before. Which made me even more
happy.

"Now it's your turn, Steve," the witch said.

Steve took the potion from the witch and
drank it.

All of a sudden Steve started to glow and
shake. And just like that he grew all of his
skin and hair back. All of the holes in his
skull, face and body started to fill in. He grew
back his eyes, nose, and ears. He straightened
up from his crooked posture, and he started
breathing again!

"Alright! I'm back!" He said.

We're so happy that we started to celebrate.

The witch invited us all to stay for some snacks before we left for home.

"Rotten flesh meatballs anyone?" she says.

We all just look at each other… Confused.

Sunday

Well, I woke up this evening in my own Zombie bed.

My room had the nice aroma of rotting flesh and smelly socks again.

My booger collection is right where I left it. Though now, it's a bit emptier thanks to Steve.

And I'm back to my twelve year old Zombie life again.

But, I'm a different Zombie now.

Being human taught me that it's not what you are on the outside that matters, but what you are on the inside that counts.

And I'm not talking about slugs, maggots, or tapeworms either.

But most of all, thanks to Eli, Steve and Alex, the biggest lesson I learned was that fitting in is not important, as long as you are willing to care for other people around you. Though they may reject you, as long as you keep on giving, you'll have all the friends you will ever need in your middle school life.

Steve said he learned some lessons too.

He even told me how proud he was of me for winning the PVP Tournament for him.

"Way to go using the secret weapon!" he said.

What secret weapon?!! I thought.

But I think for Steve, the whole experience was a just a really cool break from his normal life of punching trees and PVP Death Match Tournaments.

I mean, it's not every day you get to be a Zombie and hang out with some of the crazy Mobs from Minecraft.

Steve and the guys sent me some pics from their Dance Party too. I'm going to keep them in my Journal so that I'll never forget.

Naw, I'm really keeping them because I want to learn those dance moves.

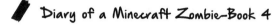

But I'm glad that it's all over.

And I'm so glad that school is almost over too.

In just a few short weeks, summer break will be here.

Which means more fun and more adventures will be waiting for me and my pals.

All I can say is that I can't wait till it gets here.

Cause I'm gonna be ready...

Bring it!

Find out What
Happens Next in...

Diary of a Minecraft Zombie Book 5
"School Daze"

Get Your Copy and Join Zombie on
More Exciting Adventures!

If you really liked this book, please tell a friend. I'm sure they will be happy you told them about it.

Leave Us a Review Too

Please support us by leaving a review. The more reviews we get the more books we will write!

Check Out All of Our Books in the Diary of a Minecraft Zombie Series

The Diary of a Minecraft Zombie Book 1
"A Scare of a Dare"

In the first book of this hilarious Minecraft adventure series, take a peek in the diary of an actual 12 year old Minecraft Zombie and all the trouble he gets into in middle school.

Get Your Copy Today!

The Diary of a Minecraft Zombie Book 2
"Bullies and Buddies"

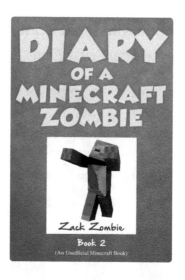

This time Zombie is up against some of the meanest and scariest mob bullies at school. Will he be able to stop the mob bullies from terrorizing him and his friends, and make it back in one piece?

Jump into the Adventure and Find Out!

The Diary of a Minecraft Zombie Book 3
"When Nature Calls"

What does a Zombie do for Spring break?
Find out in this next installment of the exciting
and hilarious adventures of a 12 year old
Minecraft Zombie!

Get Your Copy Today!

The Diary of a Minecraft Zombie Book 4
"Zombie Swap"

12 Year Old Zombie and Steve
have Switched Bodies!
Find out what happens as 12 year old
Zombie has to pretend to be human and
Steve pretends to be a zombie.

Jump into this Zany
Adventure Today!

The Diary of a Minecraft Zombie Book 5
"School Daze"

Summer Vacation is Almost Here and
12 Year Old Zombie Just Can't Wait!
Join Zombie on a Hilarious Adventure as
he tries to make it through the last few
weeks before Summer Break.

Jump into the
Adventure Today!

The Diary of a Minecraft Zombie Book 6
"Zombie Goes To Camp"

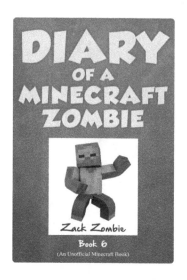

Join 12 year old Zombie, as he faces his
biggest fears, and tries to survive the next
3 weeks at Creepaway Camp.
Will he make it back in one piece?

Jump into His Crazy Summer Adventure and Find Out!

The Diary of a Minecraft Zombie Book 7
"Zombie Family Reunion"

Join Zombie and his family on their crazy
adventure as they face multiple challenges
trying to get to their 100th Year
Zombie Family Reunion.
Will Zombie even make it?

Get Your Copy Today
and Find Out!

The Diary of a Minecraft Zombie Book 8
"Back to Scare School"

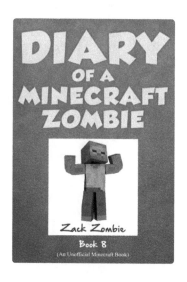

Zombie finally made it through 7th grade...
And he even made it through one really crazy
summer! But will Zombie be able to survive
through the first weeks of being an 8th grader
in Mob Scare School?

Find Out in His Latest
Adventure Today!

The Diary of a Minecraft Zombie Book 9
"Zombie's Birthday Apocalypse"

It's Halloween and it's Zombie's Birthday!
But there's a Zombie Apocalypse happening that
may totally ruin his Birthday party.Will Zombie
and his friends be able to stop the Zombie
Apocalypse so that they can finally enjoy some
cake and cookies at Zombie's Birthday Bash?

Jump into the Adventure
and Find Out!

The Diary of a Minecraft Zombie Book 10
"One Bad Apple"

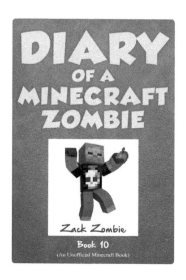

There's a new kid at Zombie's middle
school and everyone thinks he is so cool.
But the more Zombie hangs out with him, the
more trouble he gets into. Is this new Mob kid
as cool as everyone thinks he is, or is he really a
Minecraft Wolf in Sheep's clothing?

Jump Into this Zany Minecraft Adventure and Find Out!